Especially for

Margaret

From

MaryAnn

Date

Aug 8, 2010

Love You

A Touch
of Hope

Helen Steiner Rice

BARBOUR
PUBLISHING

© 2007 Helen Steiner Rice Foundation Fund, LLC, a wholly owned subsidiary of
Cincinnati Museum Center.

ISBN 978-1-61626-033-0

Devotional writing by Rebecca Currington in association with Snapdragon Group(SM)
Editorial Services.

Cover design: Greg Jackson, Thinkpen Design

Published by Barbour Publishing, Inc., P.O. Box 719, Uhrichsville, Ohio 44683,
www.barbourbooks.com

*Our mission is to publish and distribute inspirational products offering exceptional value and
biblical encouragement to the masses.*

Printed in China.

Contents

Prayer

"If you believe, you will receive whatever you ask for in prayer."

MATTHEW 21:22

It must break God's heart when He sees so many people praying to gods of stone—gods who cannot hear their pleas or help them find their way. Your God is a living God. He listens to your prayers with a heart of love. When you kneel before Him, you can feel the comforting warmth of His presence. It is then that you know you have placed your hope in the one true God— the God who hears and helps.

Just close your eyes and open your heart

And feel your worries and cares depart,

Just yield yourself to the Father above

And let Him hold you secure in His love.

So when you are tired, discouraged, and blue,

There's always one door

    that is open to you—

For the heart is a temple when God is there

As we place ourselves in His loving care.

Kneel in prayer in His presence,
  and you'll find no need to speak,
For softly in quiet communion,
  God grants you the peace
  that you seek.

For when we seek shelter
in His wondrous love,
And we ask Him to send us
help from above. . .
And that is the reason
we know it is true
That bright, shining hours
and dark, sad ones, too,
Are part of the plan
God made for each one,
And all we can pray is,
"Thy will be done."
And know that you are never alone,
For God is your Father
and you're one of His own.

Brighten your day

And lighten your way

And lessen your cares

With daily prayers.

Quiet your mind

And leave tension behind

And find inspiration

In hushed meditation.

Whenever we're troubled
and lost in despair,
We have but to seek Him
and ask Him in prayer
To guide and direct us
and help us to bear
Our sickness and sorrow,
our worry and care.

Although it sometimes seems to us
    our prayers have not been heard,
God always knows our every need
    without a single word.
And He will not forsake us,
    though the way is steep,
For always He is near to us
    a tender watch to keep. . .
And in good time He'll answer us,
    and in His love He'll send
Greater things than we have asked
    and blessings without end.

Prayers are the stairs that
lead to God, and there's
joy every step of the way
When we make our pilgrimage
to Him with love in
our hearts each day.

Whenever I am troubled and
    lost in deep despair,
I bundle all my troubles up
    and go to God in prayer. . .
I know He stilled the tempest
    and calmed the angry sea,
And I humbly ask if, in His love,
    He'll do the same for me. . .
And then I just keep quiet and
    think only thoughts of peace,
And as I abide in stillness
    my restless murmurings cease.

Prayer is so often just words unspoken,

Whispered in tears by a heart that is broken,

For God is already deeply aware

Of the burdens we find too heavy to bear...

And all we need do is seek Him in prayer

And without a word He will help us to bear

Our trials and troubles, our sickness and sorrow

And show us the way to a brighter tomorrow.

There's no need at all for impressive prayer,

For the minute we seek God He's already there.

There is only one place
    and only one Friend
Who is never too busy,
    and you can always depend
On Him to be waiting,
    with arms open wide,
To hear all the troubles
    you came to confide.
For the heavenly Father
    will always be there
When you seek Him and find
    Him at the altar of prayer.

Do not be anxious about anything,
but in everything, by prayer and petition,
with thanksgiving, present your requests to God.

PHILPPIANS 4:6

Though we feel helpless
  and alone when we start,
A prayer is the key
  that opens the heart,
And as the heart opens,
  the dear Lord comes in
And the prayer that we felt
  we could never begin
It is so easy to say,
  for the Lord understands
And He gives us new strength
  by the touch of His hands.

On the wings of prayer
   our burdens take flight,
And our load of care
   becomes bearably light,
And our heavy hearts
   are lifted above
To be healed by the balm
   of God's wonderful love.

I cannot dwell apart from You—
You would not ask or want me to,
For You have room within Your heart
To make each child of Yours a part
Of You and all Your love and care
If we but come to You in prayer.

There's no problem too big
  and no question too small—
Just ask God in faith
  and He'll answer them all—
Not always at once,
  so be patient and wait,
For God never comes too soon
  or too late. . .
So trust in His wisdom
  and believe in His Word,
For no prayer's unanswered
  and no prayer's unheard.

*"God so loved the world that he gave his one and only
Son, that whoever believes in him shall not
perish but have eternal life."*

John 3:16

Your heavenly Father has given you life, dear
friend—and not just life, but eternal life. Your
body will die and be replaced by one far better.
For those who place their hope in Him, death
holds no threat. . .no sting. It is simply a transition
from one form of life to another. He shepherds
us as we pass through the valley of the shadow of
death, proving that death really is just a shadow—
one that vanishes in the light of His presence.

Nothing really ever dies
   that is not born anew
The miracles of nature
   all tell us this is true. . .
The flowers sleeping peacefully
   beneath the winter's snow
Awaken from their icy grave when
   spring winds start to blow
And all around on every side
   new life and joy appear
To tell us nothing ever dies
   and we should have no fear,
For death is just a detour
   along life's winding way
That leads God's chosen children
   to a bright and glorious day.

Death is only a stepping-stone
To a beautiful life
   we have never known—
A place where God promised man
   he would be
Eternally happy and safe and free.

To know that life is endless
    puts new purpose in our days
And fills our hearts with
    joyous songs of hope and
    love and praise.

We all have many things to be
deeply thankful for,
But God's everlasting promise
of life forevermore
Is a reason for thanksgiving
every hour of the day
As we walk toward eternal life
along the King's highway.

Give thanks to the LORD,
for he is good.
His love endures forever.

PSALM 136:1

We cannot see the future,
   what's beyond is still unknown,
For the secret of God's kingdom
   still belongs to Him alone.
But He granted us salvation
   when His Son was crucified,
For life became immortal
   because our Savior died.

Death is a time of sleeping,
For those who die are in God's keeping,
And there's a sunrise for each soul—
For life, not death, is God's promised goal...
So trust God's promise and doubt Him never,
For only through death can man live forever.

I am the Way, so just follow Me

Though the way be rough and you cannot see...

I am the Truth which all men seek,

So heed not false prophets

   nor the words that they speak...

I am the Life, and I hold the key

That opens the door to eternity...

And in this dark world, I am the Light

To the Promised Land where there is no night.

He carried the cross to Calvary—
Carried its burden for you and me.
There on the cross He was crucified,
And because He bled and died,
We know that whatever
   our cross may be,
It leads to God and eternity.

In that fair city that God
has prepared
Are unending joys to be
happily shared
With all of our loved ones
who patiently wait
On death's other side to
open the gate.

All who believe in God's mercy and grace
Will meet their loved ones face-to-face
Where time is endless and joy unbroken
And only the words of God's love
*   are spoken.*

He who safely brought me here
Will also take me safely back.
And though in many things I lack,
He will not let me go alone
Into the valley that's unknown. . .
So I reach out and take Death's hand
And journey to the Promised Land.

Man and woman, like flowers,
    too, must sleep
Until called from the darkened deep
To live in that place where angels sing
And where there is eternal spring.

There is no night without a dawning,
　　no winter without a spring
And beyond death's dark horizon,
　　our hearts will once more sing.
For those who leave us for a while
　　have only gone away
Out of a restless, careworn world
　　into a brighter day
Where there will be no partings
　　and time is not counted by years,
Where there are no trials or troubles,
　　no worries, no cares, and no tears.

Man is but born to die and arise

For beyond this world in beauty there lies

The purpose of death, which is but to gain

Life everlasting in God's great domain…

And no one need make this journey alone,

For God has promised to take care of His own.

Live for Me and die for Me,

And I, your God, will set you free!

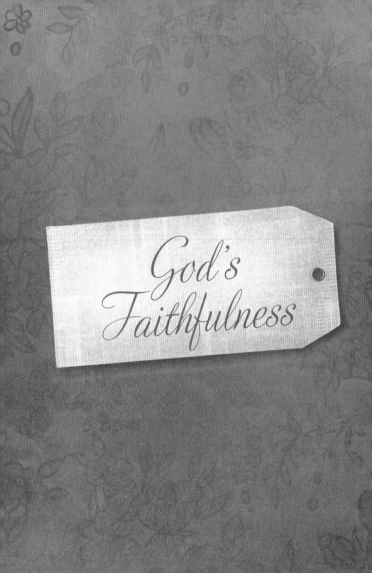

God's
Faithfulness

Your word, O LORD, is eternal; it stands firm in the heavens. Your faithfulness continues through all generations; you established the earth, and it endures.

PSALM 119:89–90

People—even those you love the most—will fail you. And you will fail them. That's how it is with human beings. But God is another story. If you put your hope in Him one hundred times, you will find Him faithful one hundred times. The more you hope in His goodness, the more you find Him utterly faithful without exception. What a wonderful thing it is to know you are trusting in the One who will never—can never—let you down.

In Thy goodness and mercy,
   look down on this weak, erring one
And tell me that I am forgiven
   for all I've so willfully done,
And teach me to humbly start
   following the path that
   the dear Savior trod
So I'll find at the end of life's journey
   a home in the city of God.

After the clouds, the sunshine,
After the winter, the spring,
After the shower, the rainbow—
For life is a changeable thing;
After the night, the morning
Bidding all darkness cease
After life's cares and sorrow,
The comfort and sweetness of peace.

Whatever our problems,
    troubles, and sorrows,
If we trust in the Lord,
    there'll be brighter tomorrows
For there's nothing too much
    for the great God to do,
And all that He asks
    or expects from you
Is faith that's unshaken
    by tribulations and tears
That keeps growing stronger
    along with the years.

Trust in His wisdom
and believe in His word,
For no prayer's unanswered
and no prayer unheard.

Now faith is being sure of what we hope for and certain of what we do not see. . . . And without faith it is impossible to please God, because anyone who comes to him must believe that he exists and that he rewards those who earnestly seek him.

Hebrews 11:1, 6

Wait with a heart that is patient for
the goodness of God to prevail—
For never do prayers go unanswered,
and His mercy and love never fail.

Cast your cares on the Lord
and he will sustain you;
he will never let the righteous fall.

Psalm 55:22

We often feel deserted in times of deep stress
Without God's presence to assure us and bless,
And it is when our senses are reeling
We realize clearly it's faith and not feeling,
For it takes great faith to patiently wait,
Believing God comes not too soon or too late.

So keep on believing
    whatever betide you,
Knowing that God will
    be with you to guide you,
And all that He promised
    will be yours to receive
If you trust Him completely
    and always believe.

The rainbow is God's promise
    of hope for you and me,
And though the clouds hang heavy
    and the sun we cannot see,
We know above the dark clouds
    that fill the stormy sky
Hope's rainbow will come shining through
    when the clouds have drifted by.

And so today I walk with God
Because I love Him so. . .
If I have faith and trust in Him
There's nothing I need know.

The Lord is our salvation
And our strength in every fight,
Our redeemer and protector,
Our eternal guiding light...
He has promised to sustain us,
He's our refuge from all harms,
And underneath this refuge
Are the everlasting arms.

"Do not store up for yourselves treasures on earth, where moth and rust destroy, and where thieves break in and steal. But store up for yourselves treasures in heaven, where moth and rust do not destroy, and where thieves do not break in and steal. For where your treasure is, there your heart will be also."

Matthew 6:19–21

The silent stars in timeless skies,

The wonderment in children's eyes,

The autumn haze, the breath of spring,

The chirping song the crickets sing,

A rosebud in a slender vase

Are all reflections of God's face.

Knowing God's love is unfailing,
and His mercy unending and great,
You have but to trust in His promise—
God comes not too soon or
too late.

When we are helpless with no place to go
And our hearts are heavy
    and our spirits are low,
If we place our lives in God's hands
And surrender completely
    to His will and demands,
The darkness lifts and the
    sun shines through,
And by His touch we are born anew.

There's truly nothing we need know
If we have faith wherever we go,
God will be there to help us bear
Our disappointments, pain, and care,
For He is our Shepherd,
    our Father, our Guide—
You're never alone
    with the Lord at your side.

God's Love

"I have loved you with an everlasting love;
I have drawn you with loving-kindness."

JEREMIAH 31:3

Human love is a wonderful thing—exciting, inspiring, intense—but often fickle. God's love, on the other hand, is constant. It never changes—solid bedrock from beginning to end. God loves you simply because you are His. He created you, and when you went astray, He brought you back at a great price. His love is based on His mercy rather than your merit. His love will remain strong today, tomorrow, and for eternity.

We are all God's children
   and He loves us, every one.
He freely and completely forgives
   all that we have done,
Asking only if we're ready
   to follow where He leads,
Content that in His wisdom
   He will answer all our needs.

What is love? No words can define it—
It's something so great
  only God could design it.
For love means much more
  than small words can express,
For what we call love is very much less
Than the beauty and depth
  and the true richness of
God's gift to mankind—
  His compassionate love.

Somebody loves you
    more than you know,
Somebody goes with you
    wherever you go,
Somebody really and truly cares
And lovingly listens to all
    of your prayers.
And if you walk in His footsteps
    and have faith to believe,
There's nothing you ask for
    that you will not receive.

His love knows no exceptions,
   so never feel excluded—
No matter who or what you are,
   your name has been included.

Kings and kingdoms all pass away—
Nothing on earth endures. . .
But the love of God who sent His Son
Is forever and ever yours!

The sky and the stars, the waves and the sea,
The dew on the grass, the leaves on the tree
Are constant reminders of God
    and His nearness,
Proclaiming His presence with crystal-like
    clearness.
So how could I think God was far, far away
When I feel Him beside me every hour
    of the day?
And I've plenty of reasons to know
    God's my friend,
And this is one friendship that time
    cannot end!

God's love is like an island
    in life's ocean vast and wide—
A peaceful, quiet shelter
    from the restless, rising tide.
God's love is like a fortress,
    and we seek protection there
When the waves of tribulation
    seem to drown us in despair.

God's love is like a sanctuary where
  our souls can find sweet rest
From the struggle and the tension of
  life's fast and futile quest.
God's love is like a beacon burning
  bright with faith and prayer,
And through the changing scenes of
  life we can find a haven there.

Be imitators of God, therefore,
as dearly loved children
and live a life of love.

Ephesians 5:1–2

No matter what your past has been,
Trust God to understand.
And no matter what your problem is
Just place it in His hand—
For in all of our unloveliness
This great God loves us still.
He loved us since the world began
And what's more, He always will.

What more can we ask of our Father
Than to know we are never alone,
That His mercy and love are unfailing,
And He makes all our problems
  His own.

Friendship
and Love

Whoever loves his brother lives in the light,
and there is nothing in him to make him stumble.

1 JOHN 2:10

The miracle of God's love for us is more than
we could ever have asked or imagined, and yet
He has given above and beyond. He has given
us friends to warm our hearts and stand beside
us in the good times and the bad, to bring us
hope and encouragement. God revels in the
love we have for each other and encourages,
even commands, us to love each other as He
has loved us. What a generous God we serve.

Among the great and glorious gifts
    our heavenly Father sends
Is the gift of understanding that
    we find in loving friends,
For it's not money or gifts or material things,
But understanding the joy it brings,
That can change this old world
    in wonderful ways
And put goodness and mercy
    back in our days.

Friendship is a priceless gift
That can't be bought or sold,
But to have an understanding friend
Is worth far more than gold.

Thank you for your friendship
And your understanding of
The folks who truly love you
And the folks you truly love.

Friends and prayers are

priceless treasures

Beyond all monetary measures,

And so I say a special prayer

That God will keep you in His care.

Like ships upon the sea of life
  we meet with friends so dear,
Then sail on swiftly from the ones
  we'd like to linger near;
Sometimes I wish the winds would cease,
  the waves be quiet, too,
And let me sort of drift along
  beside a friend like you.

Just like a sunbeam brightens the sky,

A smile on the face of a passerby

Can make a drab and crowded street

A pleasant place where

two smiles meet.

Rejoice in the Lord always.

I will say it again: Rejoice!

Philippians 4:4

The more of everything
   you share,
The more you'll always
   have to spare. . .
For only what you give away
Enriches you from day to day!

There are things we cannot measure,
Like the depths of waves and sea
And the heights of stars in heaven
And the joy you bring to me...
Like eternity's long endlessness
And the sunset's golden hue,
There is no way to measure
The love I have for you.

An unlit candle gives no light,
Only when it's burning is it
    shining bright.
And life is empty, dull, and dark,
Until doing things for others gives
    the needed spark
That sets a useless life on fire
And fills the heart with new desire.

Friendship, like flowers, blooms
   ever more fair
When carefully tended by dear
   friends who care;
And life's lovely garden would be
   sweeter by far
If all who passed through it were
   as nice as you are.

Every day's a good day to lose
  yourself in others
And any time a good time to see
  mankind as brothers,
And this can only happen when
  you realize it's true
That everyone needs someone
  and that someone is you.

Across the years we've met in dreams
And shared each other's hopes and
   schemes,
We knew a friendship rich and rare
And beauty far beyond compare.
Then you reached out your arms for more,
To catch what you were yearning for.
But little did you think or guess
That one can't capture happiness
Because it's unrestrained and free,
Unfettered by reality.

We rob ourselves of life's greatest need

When we lock up our hearts and fail to heed

The outstretched hand, reaching to find

A kindred spirit whose heart and mind

Are lonely and longing to somehow share

Our joys and sorrows and to make us aware

That life's completeness and richness depends

On the things we share with our loved ones
    and friends.

Gold is cold and lifeless,
　　it cannot see nor hear,
And in your times of trouble,
　　it is powerless to cheer.
It has no ears to listen,
　　no heart to understand.
It cannot bring you comfort
　　or reach out a helping hand.
So when you ask God for a gift,
　　be thankful if He sends
Not diamonds, pearls, or riches,
　　but the love of real, true friends.

If people like me didn't know
    people like you,
Life would lose its meaning and
    its richness, too.
For the friends that we make
    are life's gifts of love,
And I think friends are sent
    right from heaven above.
And thinking of you somehow
    makes me feel
That God is love and He's
    very real.

In this world of trouble that
   is filled with anxious care,
Everybody needs a friend in
   whom they're free to share,
The little secret heartaches that
   lay heavy on the mind,
We seek our true and trusted friend
   in the knowledge that we'll find
A heart that's sympathetic and
   an understanding mind.

Like roses in a garden,
    kindness fills the air
With a certain bit of sweetness
    as it touches everywhere.
For kindness is a circle that never,
    never ends
But just keeps ever-widening
    in the circle of our friends.
For the more you give, the more
    you get is proven every day,
And so to get the most from life
    you must give yourself away.

You're like a ray of sunshine
Or a star up in the sky,
You add a special brightness
Whenever you pass by.
For In this raucous, restless world
We're small but God is great,
And in His love, dear friend,
Our hearts communicate!

Father, make us kind and wise

So we may always recognize

The blessings that are ours to take,

The friendships that are ours to make,

If we but open our heart's door wide

To let the sunshine of love inside.

Nothing on earth can make
life more worthwhile
Than a true, loyal friend and
the warmth of a smile,
For, just like a sunbeam makes
the cloudy days brighter,
The smile of a friend makes a
heavy heart lighter.

Courage

"This is my command—be strong and courageous!
Do not be afraid or discouraged. For the LORD
your God is with you wherever you go."

JOSHUA 1:9 NLT

Does your heart feel faint with fear when faced
with the challenges of this life? The truth is,
we all have fainting hearts—even the biggest,
bravest people among us. But we need not fear
anything when God is on our side. Our courage
is not vested in our limited capabilities but in
His mighty power. Our heavenly Father fights
for us. Place your faith and your hope in Him.

Blessed are the people
   who learn to accept
The trouble men try to
   escape and reject,
For in our acceptance
   we're given great grace
And courage and faith
   and the strength to face
The daily troubles
   that come to us all,
So we may learn to stand
   straight and tall.

Wrapped within His kindness
you are sheltered and secure
And under His direction
your way is safe and sure.

They tell me that prayer
    helps to quiet the mind
And to unburden the heart,
    for in stillness we find
A newborn assurance
    that Someone does care
And Someone does answer
    each small, sincere prayer!

In this age of unrest,
  with danger all around,
We need Thy hand to lead us
  to higher, safer ground. . .
We need Thy help and counsel
  to make us more aware
That our safety and security
  lie solely in Thy care.

Give us strength and courage
　　to be honorable and true
Practicing Your precepts
　　in everything we do.
And keep us gently humble
　　in the greatness of Thy love
So someday we are fit to dwell
　　with Thee in peace above.

When seen through God's eyes,
    earthly troubles diminish,
And we're given new strength
    to face and to finish
Life's daily tasks
    as they come along,
If we but pray for strength
    to keep us strong.

Let us then approach the throne of grace
with confidence, so that we may receive mercy
and find grace to help us in our time of need.

Hebrews 4:16

You are ushering in another day
   untouched and freshly new
So here I come to ask You, God,
   if You'll renew me, too.
And Father, I am well aware
   I can't make it on my own,
So take my hand and hold it tight,
   for I can't walk alone.

Always remember, the hills ahead
    are never as steep as they seem,
And with faith in your heart
    start upward and climb till you
    reach your dream.
Though the way ahead seems steep
Be not afraid, for He will keep
Tender watch through night and day
And He will hear each prayer you pray.

Cast your burden on Him, seek
His counsel when distressed,
And go to Him for comfort when
you're lonely and oppressed—
For God is our encouragement
in troubles and in trials,
And in suffering and in sorrow
He will turn our tears to smiles.

Growing trees are strengthened
　　when they withstand the storm,
And the sharp cut of a chisel
　　gives the marble grace and form.
God never hurts us needlessly
　　and He never wastes our pain,
For every loss He sends to us
　　is followed by rich gain.
So whenever we are troubled
　　and when everything goes wrong,
It is just God working in us
　　to make our spirits strong.

Nothing is ever too hard to do
If your faith is strong and your
    purpose is true...
So never give up and never stop,
Just journey on to the mountaintop.

God, grant me. . .

Courage and hope for every day,

Faith to guide me along my way

Understanding and wisdom, too,

And grace to accept what life

gives me to do.

Faith

Jesus said to the disciples, "Have faith in God. I tell you the truth, you can say to this mountain, 'May you be lifted up and thrown into the sea,' and it will happen."

MARK 11:22–23 NLT

While faith and hope are twin virtues—both affect how we receive from God—they have at least one big difference. While hope is quiet, patient, and accustomed to waiting, faith speaks out, takes action, and moves mountains. Both are God's gifts to equip us for successful lives here on earth. Hope in God, dear friend, then invest your faith in His precious promises. It's a winning combination.

Faith to believe
    when the way is rough
And faith to hang on
    when the going is tough
Will never fail to pull us through
And bring us strength
    and comfort, too.

Faith makes it wholly possible
to quietly endure
The violent world around us
for in God we are secure.

Though I cannot find Your hand
To lead me on to the Promised Land,
I still believe with all my being
Your hand is there beyond my seeing.

All who have God's blessing
can rest safely in His care,
For He promises safe passage
on the wings of faith and prayer.

Let us fix our eyes on Jesus, the author and perfecter of our faith.

Hebrews 12:2

Faith is a force that is greater
Than knowledge or power or skill. . .
And the darkest defeat
   turns to triumph
If we trust in God's wisdom
   and will.

Take heart and meet each minute
with faith in God's great love,
Aware that every day of life
is controlled by God above...
And never dread tomorrow
or what the future brings—
Just pray for strength and courage
and trust God in all things.

When the darkness shuts out the light,

We must lean on faith to restore our sight,

For there is nothing we need to know

If we have faith that wherever we go

God will be there to help us bear

Our disappointments, pain, and care.

Faith in things we cannot see
Requires a child's simplicity.
For faith alone can save man's soul
And lead him to a higher goal,
For there's but one
  unfailing source—
We win by faith and not by force.

No day is too dark and no burden too great

That God in His love cannot penetrate...

And to know and believe without

   question or doubt

That no matter what happens

   God is there to help out

Is to hold in your hand the golden key

To peace and joy and serenity.

For with patience to wait
and faith to endure,
Your life will be blessed
and your future secure,
For God is but testing
your faith and your love
Before He appoints you
to rise far above
All the small things
that so sorely distress you,
For God's only intention is to
strengthen and bless you.

It's easy to grow downhearted
    when nothing goes your way.
It's easy to be discouraged
    when you have a troublesome day.
But trouble is only a challenge
    to spur you on to achieve
The best that God has to offer
    if you have the faith to believe.

Sometimes when faith is running low
And I cannot fathom why things are so. . .
I walk alone among the flowers I grow
And learn the answers
    to all I would know. . .
For among my flowers I have come to see
Life's miracle and its mystery. . .
And standing in silence and reverie
My faith comes flooding back to me.

When our hearts are heavy
    with worry and care
And we are lost in the depths of despair...
That is the time when faith alone
Can lead us out of the dark unknown.
For faith to believe when the way is rough
And faith to hang on when the going is tough
Will never fail to pull us through
And bring us strength and comfort, too.

With faith, let go and let
  God lead the way
Into a brighter and
  less-troubled day.
For God has a plan for everyone,
If we learn to pray,
  "Thy will be done."

All we really ever need
Is faith as a grain of mustard seed,
For all God asks is
   do you believe—
For if you do, you shall receive.

No one discovers the fullness
    or the greatness of God's love
Unless they have walked in the darkness
    with only a light from above.
For the faith to endure whatever comes
    is born of sorrow and trials
And strengthened only by discipline
    and nurtured by self-denials.
So be not disheartened by troubles,
    for trials are the building blocks
On which to erect a fortress of faith
    secure on God's ageless rocks.

Faith is a force that is greater
Than knowledge or power or skill,
And many defeats turn to triumphs
If you trust in God's wisdom and will.
For faith is a mover of mountains—
There's nothing that God cannot do—
So start out today with
    faith in your heart,
And climb till your dreams come true.

We are hard pressed on every side,
but not crushed; perplexed, but not in
despair; persecuted, but not abandoned;
struck down, but not destroyed.

2 Corinthians 4:8–9

Renewal

*My health may fail, and my spirit may
grow weak, but God remains the strength
of my heart; he is mine forever.*

PSALM 73:26 NLT

Like a charger hooked up to a battery, the Holy
Spirit dwells within us, renewing us day by day.
Renewal is not something to save for a
retreat; God designed it to be a constant,
keeping us always in tune with Him and His
purpose for our lives. When the world around
you is especially harsh, when your heart is ready
to break and you wonder if all is lost, look
inside. Ask the Holy Spirit to restore your hope.

Thank You, God, for the beauty
around me everywhere,
The gentle rain and glistening dew,
the sunshine and the air,
The joyous gift of feeling
the soul's soft, whispering voice
That speaks to me from deep within
and makes my heart rejoice.

There is no night without dawning,
No winter without a spring,
And beyond death's dark horizon
Our hearts once more will sing.

Cast your burden on Him,
    seek His counsel when distressed,
And go to Him for comfort
    when you're lonely and oppressed.
For God is our encouragement
    in troubles and in trials,
And in suffering and in sorrow
    He will turn our tears to smiles.

Hope for a world grown cynically cold,
Hungry for power and greedy for gold—
Faith to believe when, within and without,
There's a nameless fear in a world of doubt—
Love that is bigger than race or creed
To cover the world and fulfill each need.

You are so great. . .
We are so small. . .
And when trouble comes
    as it does to us all
There's so little that we can do
Except to place our trust in You.

Open your heart's door
    and let Christ come in,
And He'll give you new life
    and free you from sin—
And there is no joy
    that can ever compare
With the joy of knowing
    you're in God's care.

For it is by grace you have been saved, through faith—and this not from yourselves, it is the gift of God—not by works, so that no one can boast.

EPHESIANS 2:8–9

Why am I cast down and despondently sad
When I long to be happy
    and joyous and glad?
Why is my heart heavy with
    unfathomable weight
As I try to escape this soul-saddened state?
And then, with God's help
    it all becomes clear,
The soul has its seasons
    just the same as the year.
But meeting these seasons of dark desolation
With strength that is born of anticipation
That comes from knowing that
    autumn-time sadness
Will surely be followed by a
    springtime of gladness.

I see the dew glisten
  in crystal-like splendor
While God, with a touch
  that is gentle and tender,
Wraps up the night and
  softly tucks it away
And hangs out the sun
  to herald a new day. . .
And so I give thanks
  and my heart kneels to pray,
"God, keep me and guide me
  and go with me today."

In prayer there is renewal of
    the spirit, mind, and heart
For everything is lifted up
    in which God has a part. . .
For when we go to God in prayer
    our thoughts are rearranged,
So even though our problems
    have not been solved or changed,
Somehow the good Lord gives us
    the power to understand
That He who holds tomorrow
    is the One who holds our hand.

You walk with me and talk with me,

For I am Yours eternally,

And when I stumble, slip, and fall

Because I'm weak and lost and small,

You help me up and take my hand

And lead me toward the

Promised Land.

When your heart is heavy
　　and your day is full with care,
Instead of trying to escape,
　　why not withdraw in prayer?
For in prayer there is renewal
　　of the spirit, mind, and heart,
For everything is lifted up
　　in which God has a part.

His goodness is unfailing,
   His kindness knows no end,
For the Lord is a good Shepherd
   on whom you can depend.
He will guard and guide and keep you
   in His loving, watchful care,
And when traveling in dark valleys,
   your Shepherd will be there.

When I open up my eyes
   to greet another day,
I'll find myself renewed in strength
   and there will open up a way
To meet what seemed impossible
   for me to solve alone,
And once again I'll be assured
   I am never on my own.

God grant these gifts of faith,
   hope, and love—
Three things this world
   has so little of—
For only these gifts
   from our Father above
Can turn our hearts
   from hatred to love.

Deliverance
from Trials

You are my hiding place; you will protect me from
trouble and surround me with songs of deliverance.

Psalm 32:7

As children we were eager to take steps out into the world; but as soon as we met the unexpected, we ran right back to our parents. They were the safe place where we could hide from those things that frightened us. God promises that we can run to Him at any age. When your trials and tribulations overwhelm you, look to Him for deliverance. Make Him your safe place. He will surround you with peace.

When life seems empty
　　and there's no place to go,
When your heart is troubled
　　and your spirits are low,
The burden that seems
　　too heavy to bear
God lifts away on the
　　wings of prayer.

God in His goodness has promised that

the cross that He gives us to wear

Will never exceed our endurance or

be more than our strength can bear.

Secure in a blessed assurance
we can smile as we face tomorrow,
For God holds the key to the future,
and no sorrow or care
we need borrow.

What more can we ask of the Savior
Than to know we are never alone—
That His mercy and love are unfailing
And He makes all our
   problems His own.

"And surely I am with you always,
to the very end of the age."

MATTHEW 28:20

Sometimes the road of life seems long
as we travel through the years
And with a heart that's broken
and eyes brimful of tears,
We falter in our weariness
and sink beside the way.
But God leans down and whispers,
"Child, there'll be another day."
And the road will grow much
smoother and much easier to face,
So do not be disheartened—
this is just a resting place.

Wish not for the easy way
    to win your heart's desire,
For the joy's in overcoming
    and withstanding flood and fire—
For to triumph over trouble
    and grow stronger with defeat
Is to win the kind of victory
    that will make your life complete.

When the fires of life
   burn deep in your heart
And the winds of destruction
   seem to tear you apart,
Remember God loves you
   and wants to protect you.
So seek that small haven
   and be guided by prayer
To that place of protection
   within God's loving care.

He will not let me go alone

Into the valley that's unknown.

Kings and kingdoms all pass away—

Nothing on earth endures.

But the love of God who sent His Son

Is forever and ever yours.

God, be my resting place
   and my protection
In hours of trouble, defeat,
   and dejection—
May I never give way to
   self-pity and sorrow,
May I always be sure
   of a better tomorrow,
May I stand undaunted,
   come what may,
Secure in the knowledge
   I have only to pray
And ask my Creator
   and Father above
To keep me serene
   in His grace and His love.

Teach us that it takes the showers
to make the flowers grow,
And only in the storms of life
when the winds of trouble blow
Can man, too, reach maturity
and grow in faith and grace
And gain the strength and courage
to enable him to face
Sunny days as well as rain,
high peaks as well as low,
Knowing that the April showers
will make the May flowers grow. . .
And then at last may we accept
the sunshine and the showers,
Confident it takes them both
to make salvation ours.

When you're troubled and worried
   and sick at heart
And your plans are upset and
   your world falls apart,
Remember God's ready and waiting to share
The burden you find too heavy to bear.
So with faith, let go and let God lead the way
Into a brighter and less troubled day.

There are times when life overwhelms
   us and our trials seem too
   many to bear—
It is then we should stop to remember
   God is standing by, ready to share
The uncertain hours that confront us
   and fill us with fear and despair.

My blessings are so many,
My troubles are so few,
How can I feel discouraged
When I know that I have You?
And I have the sweet assurance
That I'll never stand alone
If I but keep remembering
I am Yours and Yours alone.

I am often weak and weary, and life
    is dark and bleak and dreary. . .
But somehow when I realize that
    He who made the sea and skies
And holds the whole world in His hand
    has my small soul in His command,
It gives me strength to try once more
    to somehow reach the heavenly door
Where I will live forevermore with
    friends and loved ones I adore.

Fulfillment

A cheerful heart is good medicine,
but a crushed spirit dries up the bones.

PROVERBS 17:22

God has a plan for you, dear friend. His plan includes hope, faith, courage, blessing, and much more. He is determined to fulfill His plan in your life. Ask Him to open your eyes to all He has provided for you, to show you the purpose for which you were created. Fulfillment doesn't come from scholarly degrees, human success, financial prosperity, or any other earthly accomplishment. It comes from knowing and doing the will of God.

For as the flowering branches
    depend upon the tree
To nourish and fulfill them
    till they reach maturity,
We, too, must be dependent
    on our Father up above,
For we are but the branches
    and He's the tree of love.

When we "give ourselves away"
in sacrifice and love,
We are laying up rich treasures
in God's kingdom up above.

Carry each other's burdens, and in this

way you will fulfill the law of Christ.

GALATIANS 6:2

Any sacrifice on earth made
in the dear Lord's name,
Assures the giver of a place
in heaven's hall of fame.

In prayer there is renewal
  of the spirit, mind, and heart
For everything is lifted up
  in which God has a part. . .
For when we go to God in prayer
  our thoughts are rearranged,
So even though our problems
  have not been solved or changed,
Somehow the good Lord gives us
  the power to understand
That He who holds tomorrow
  is the One who holds our hand.

Each day there are showers of blessings

Sent from the Father above,

For God is a great, lavish giver,

And there is no end to His love.

No matter how big man's dreams are,

God's blessings are infinitely more,

For always God's giving is greater

Than what man is asking for.

Kneel in prayer in His presence
And you'll find no need to speak,
For softly in silent communion
God grants you the peace
   that you seek.

Father, make us kind and wise

So we may always recognize

The blessings that are ours to take,

The friendships that are ours to make.

Withdrawal means renewal
if we withdraw to pray
And listen in the quietness
to hear what God will say.

*Come near to God and he
will come near to you.*

JAMES 4:8

If we put our problems in God's hand,
There is nothing we need understand…
It is enough to just believe
That what we need we will receive.

Dear God, You are a part of me—
You're all I do and all I see,
You're what I say and what I do,
For all my life belongs to You.

Good health, good humor,
And good sense,
No one is poor
With this defense.

Each day at dawning I lift my heart high
And raise up my eyes to the infinite sky,
I watch the night vanish as a new day is born,
And I hear the birds sing
    on the wings of the morn;
I see the dew glisten in crystal-like splendor
While God, with a touch
    that is gentle and tender,
Wraps up the night and softly tucks it away
And hangs out the sun to herald a new day.

America's beloved inspirational poet laureate, **Helen Steiner Rice**, has encouraged millions of people through her beautiful and uplifting verse. Born in Lorain, Ohio, in 1900, Helen was the daughter of a railroad man and an accomplished seamstress and began writing poetry at a young age.

In 1918, Helen began working for a public utilities company and eventually became one of the first female advertising managers and public speakers in the country. In January 1929, she married a wealthy banker named Franklin Rice, who later sank into depression during the Great Depression and eventually committed suicide. Helen later said that her suffering made her sensitive to the pain of others. Her sadness helped her to write some of her most uplifting verses.

Her work for a Cincinnati, Ohio, greeting card company eventually led to her nationwide popularity as a poet when her Christmas card poem "The Priceless Gift of Christmas" was first read on the *Lawrence Welk Show*. Soon Helen had produced several books of her poetry that were a source of inspiration to millions of readers.

Helen died in 1981, leaving a foundation in her name to offer assistance to the needy and the elderly. Now more than twenty-five years after her death, Helen's words still speak powerfully to the hearts of readers about love and comfort, faith and hope, peace and joy.